Rites of Passage

Rose MK

BookLeaf Publishing

India | USA | UK

Presentation by *BookLeaf Publishing*

Web: www.bookleafpub.com

E-mail: info@bookleafpub.com

ISBN: 9789360945800

First edition 2024

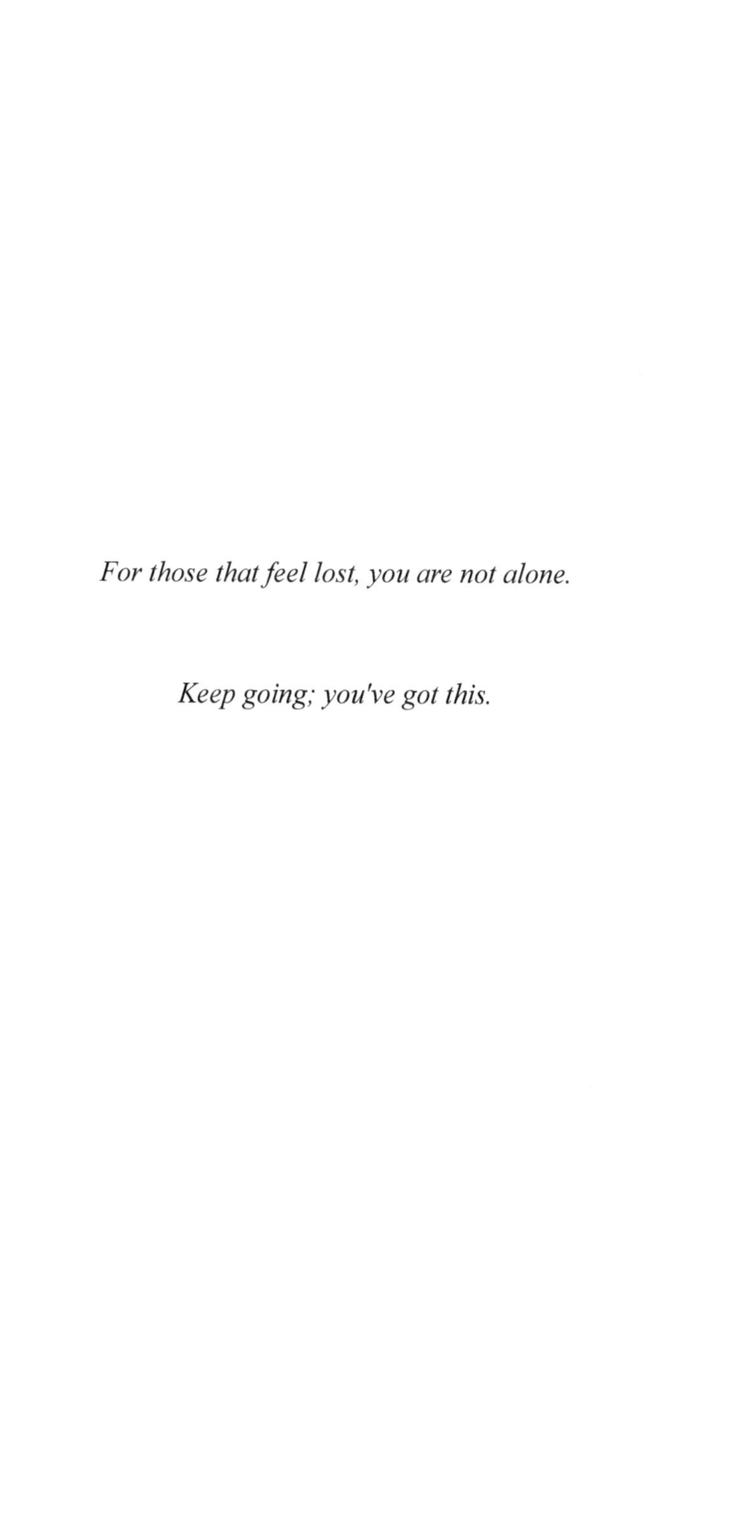

For those that feel lost, you are not alone.

Keep going; you've got this.

ACKNOWLEDGEMENT

There are several people that deserve thanks for their inspiration and support of me during the writing of this book.

Firstly, I would like to thank all of the magnificent poets that have inspired me to write. Without their beautiful words to fill me head, I surely would have none to give.

My husband, Loz, you been an avid supporter of my writing for many years. You have encouraged me time and time again to write, and I finally did it. You make me believe I can speak to anything I have a voice for, and that is something special. Thank you.

To my family, you have been the subject of some of this work, so apologies for that. In all seriousness though, even if a piece is not directly about you, there are fibres of you woven throughout this book because ultimately, you are the threads that make up the tapestry of my life, and so you are integral to this book and what it has to say.

There has to be a big shout out and thank you to all the students I have taught over the years. You have truly inspired me, and although it is a cliché, you've kept me young. You allow me to reflect deeply own my own childhood when you ask me to help you navigate yours. Hopefully, I've helped. You are fabulous young people, and I have no doubt, will do something wonderful with the years that lie ahead of you. Do not waste them- they are precious.

Finally, thank you to those at BookLeaf Publishing that have helped breathe life into this collection of poems. Without you, it would not be possible. Thank you so much for this opportunity.

PREFACE

When deciding to write a collection of poetry, I'll be honest, I wasn't entirely sure what I wanted to say. What profound sentiment would I, the country girl from Somerset, have to share with the world? Then it dawned on me that I have never engaged in the art of poetry to say something profound. In fact, it has often been to say something simple, something raw, something that needed to be said for my own personal growth and nothing more. So, when I finally put pen to paper, that was at the forefront of my mind.

Most of my poetry therefore, stems from my personal experiences, and so this body of work would need do the same. It had to be words that reflected my personal experiences but also link to the universal rites that we all connect with.

I was heavily inspired by the young people I teach and also the family around me. They are all at very different stages of their lives, and they have something to say about the rites that they have endured, and so I tried to channel that in this collection. I hope that whoever reads this finds something that they relate to, something to give them hope, or allow them to see the beauty in the absurdity of life.

Meeting On The Margins

We met for the first time,
On the margins of life and death,
Both of us screaming for life

and so began a life of screaming.
A constant pull at the balance between us,
Subtle shifts that were earthquakes in our core.

A chasm formed in our need to be heard,
Our words, tempests, unleashed upon the other
in spite of prior storms.

Just like waves atop the unforgiving ocean,
Came great swells of devastation,
Leaving a shipwreck of our love.

Thunder and lightning,
Would carve our path onward
for many years, electric, dangerous.

All the while a volcano no longer dormant,
From the depths of us,
Ripped through the landscape of our life.

A scorched earth was all that was left,

Both of us broken, burnt, and scarred,
We lay down in ash.

Breaking through the still-smoking surface,
A green and tender sapling,
Sets out its leaves in hopeful anticipation.

Eternal Conflict

Babies are a source of joy,
The apple of someone's eye,
Whether they are a girl or boy,
They're a diamond in the sky.

It's just not the way it is for me,
There's no broodiness to share,
I hold a selfishness you see,
The thought is too tough to bare.

To travel,
To love,
To be spontaneous,
Free.
These are all the selfish thoughts that live in the
heart of me.

But as I get older,
And the years pass me by,
My conscience grows bolder,
I ask myself why?

What is the point,
In a life without being 'mum'?
Is this just another way

For me to be number one?

I have no answers to these questions,
No deep and burning need,
Just a thought of distant regret,
Or the growth of some small seed.

This is wryly amusing,
It's something quite ironic,
Expecting to find peace,
But no, an eternal conflict.

Righteous Rebellion

I am going where you said I shouldn't,
In fact, you said I couldn't,
And I believe you thought I wouldn't.

So, here I am,
One foot in the dirt,
Headed in a direction that you think will hurt.

While your fear is screaming,
My heart is wildly dreaming,
As I take another step.

This way will take twice as long,
Be twice as tough,
And you will remind me twice as much about
just how tough it is.

However, much like ginger,
Some things that don't look appealing,
Hold much needed healing.

I will skip, trip, and fall,
Face first in the earth,
But it will be a blessing, a rebirth.

The rough terrain of life for me is no match,
I am a truck,
Ploughing through when I find myself stuck.

I am the whole,
Of the two halves of you,
Oh, the things that I can do.

Chopped Locks

Every child loves scissors,
Scissors are the best,
But mostly kids love scissors,
When they put them to the test.

They test them on their Barbies,
And on their teddies too,
But testing them on themselves,
Is their favourite thing to do!

Chopping off their fringes,
Hacking chunks of hair,
Chopping off their locks
until there's very little there.

Why they hide the scissors,
Or the newly chopped off hair,
It boggles every parent,
As they stand in shock and stare

at the living abstract artwork,
That is their child's new look,
And question their life choices,
Knowing this too is one they took.

Because every child loves scissors,
And that's including you,
So do not preach to children,
For they know not what they do.

The First of Many

Unrelenting anxiety,
Dry lips and unkempt hair,
All wrapped up in a young boy playing Man.

You both were perched on the edge,
Of a wall by a railway line,
Listening to the rhythmic runs of passing trains.

You knew it was coming,
Your eyes plead longingly,
Hers averted your gaze.

Empty, dead words,
Consumed the space around your head,
She, more alive with each release.

Breaching the void,
Your shaking hand moves for hers,
Avoidance. Her final disconnect.

Heavy tears to be met
with heavy sighs,
A true death.

The first of many.

Leaving

It is nearly here,
The time for you to sink or swim,
The time to face your fears,
To live as winter wolves in play,
And embrace the silence, the tears.

If I can teach you something about
knowing love and pain,
You must meet with them both equally,
For they measure just the same.

Traversing life will be hard,
When you just want to be free,
I still reckon it's worth it,
To see how brave you can be.

Like wild bluebells you'll bloom,
Oh, how beautiful you'll be,
Glowing as if lit by a thousand suns,
Or when moonlight touches the sea.

You'll be far from an expert,
But it's easier than you think,
Even on days when you've got nothing to give,
When you might be on the brink.

You'll learn this for yourself, one day,
Staring up at a summer moon,
When the stars look down with wondrous eyes,
And your childhood's gone too soon.

Like young wild fawns I've loved you,
Like strong wild stags you'll leave,
To learn hard lessons that life has to teach,
And in the wilderness finally breathe.

(Weekly) Rapture

You swear to gods you
don't believe in,
That you'll never drink again,
As you purge your sins into a bin.

Later, in poses of supplication,
Before your ivory shrine,
You profess your love for me,
As I am the saviour of your tangled mane.

Praying for your world to stop spinning,
I tuck you into fresh sheets,
Adorn you in clean PJs,
Place a glass of holy water by your bed.

A baptism complete,
You awake to preach to me,
Of how you are a changed woman.
You've turned from wine to water for good.

But we both know this hymn
Is one you'll sing again next week.

Him

A monster took his deepest insecurities,
Held me down,
And made me take them,
Then he smacked the love right out of me.
Made sure that I stayed small,
Enough to never leave,
Because who would want me?
Erased everything that made him love me
Until he didn't love me,
Because just look at me,
Disgusting.

I rejoice at the thought,
That cornered animals fight,
Knowing I did exactly that.
I fought for myself,
The girl that deserved to be loved.
She needed me,
Wanted me, and loved me,
Like he never could.
Never again,
Will I be tamed by someone so monstrous as
him.

Words Fail Me

That tainted smile smeared across your face
holds warmth in a cold kind of way.
I meet with your eyes,
It's no surprise to find the place where love dies.

I clutch at my chest as you kill me with ease,
In my head I fall to my knees,
But no, I stand in silence. Wish I'd spoken.
You're trying to break something that's already
broken.

Hope is not lost but it's fading fast,
As we transform from present to past.
I know I've got something to say,
It's just finding the way

to stop the tears my eyes chase,
Hide the pain that's punched on my face.
Words I wished for fail to arrive,
My weakened happiness runs to survive.

Staring at the blackened ground,
Pondering if what's lost can be found.
It can't, and I'm done,
There's no war here to be won.

Wrapped up in crisp cold sheets,
Pleading the night for sleep.
Soon enough though you're wept away,
Tomorrow bares a gift: a bright new day.

Commute

Awkward silences,
Broken by awkward smiles.

Our eyes connect,
Closing the distance between us.

Warmth emanates from your soul to mine,
And I feel it.

The air becomes heavy,
Closing in on me.

I'm done. Taken.
So are you.

We have never spoken,
Pulling the words from the edge of my mind,
I move.

Grinding to a halt,
The train stops.

Time to leave,
Until tomorrow.

Marriage

Marriage is the every day,
the small things that you do,
It's the going out of your way,
To support the both of you.

Marriage is not a delight,
Sometimes it might be tense,
Though by the fall of night,
You'll find your common sense.

Marriage is a vow you make,
To stay both strong and true,
To give more than you'll ever take,
And see your promise through.

It is two souls binding themselves together,
Knowing true love, always and forever.

Yield

Armoured with hardened hearts for shields,
Holding swords made of our deepest fears,
We fight.
Steel on steel,
Our back and forth of insults cut deep,
The exhaustion is overwhelming,
The stubborn nature residing in us two means,
We do not rest.

These wounds will not heal,
If we do not put down our swords and think
forward,
We will lay waste to what we have,
Lay waste to what could be,
Taking in our life we turned a battlefield,
We stop. We cry. We yield.

Unpacking

Boxes are for many things,
Tissues, rings, appliances,
and feelings.

We're so good at packing,
Keeping things tidy,
Nobody notices,

Just how much is in that box.

We have watched others,
Watched them for years,
And we have learned.

We've packed things so tight,
No wasted space and
double strength tape.

We occasionally look,
To remember what's inside,
That bloody box.

The box might break,
So we take our time
to pull out each feeling.

They're so ugly and broken,
We unpacked too quickly
and now it's a mess.

We pack them back up,
Slinging in the shame
that's just arrived.

That box is sealed,
And awaits a time,
When we're ready to deal with

just how much is in that box.

Mirror

The mirror speaks truths I am not prepared for,
That I am no longer young,
That I have yet another line in my face,
And the coffee I insist on consuming has stained
my teeth.

The gall of this mirror knows no bounds,
As it highlights the lack of sleep stamped under
each eye,
Claims my brows have more in common with
caterpillars than I think,
And that the fake lashes I apply are but the
spiders of my eyes.

The audacity of this mirror as it reflects,
That pink lipstick is for the young - and those
without stained teeth,
And all the waters of the Nile could not quench
this skin,
for I am aging.

One day, it looks at me for a long time,
And scathes that my attempts to conceal and
cover up,

What I have wrought upon this face are
insulting.

I look back at the mirror for a long time,
And speak truths that it is not prepared for,
That a trove of life is mapped across my skin,
And that it should take more time to appreciate,
All that it has weathered for me.

Found

It felt like I was taking full breaths
for the very first time,
Like a fresh winter walk
after days of solemn rain,
As though I plunged full weight
into cold water in a heatwave.

That's how it felt when I finally found myself.

Revelations

Know that Birds are beautiful,
Food cooked over many hours is the best
and so is food shared with many people.
Books are treasure,
Plants are life,
And watching them grow and bloom
even when lacking water brings us hope.
Tea is a human right, surely,
And being alone is not the same as being lonely,
Laughter is a great medicine for anything thing
that ails you,
And kitchen dancing is what freedom tastes like.
Realising that life is made of such trivial
pursuits,
Might ease the weight of yours that you
are so sure you want to carry.

Body

Touch has always come easy to you,
Your hands will gladly clasp others,
Will soothe your child,
Will comfort a friend.

Your backbone has toughened,
Armoured to take the weight and burden of life.
It has held everything together,
Even yourself at times.

When your back gives in,
Your elbows fight forward,
Stubborn and strong.
You make a path where there isn't one.

Your legs take you along,
Keep you moving and hold you up,
Trudging onward when others would fall,
Taking you to places others will never see.

A blessing in disguise,
Remember this,
Your body has and will support you through it
all.

Lop-Eared Love

Your tippy-tapping of feet,
Scattered moves on the offbeat,
The sleeping heavily all day,
Huffing through your whiskers grey,
Remind me of your age,
My little lop-eared love.

There is a clouding in your eye,
There is a limping that I spy,
You no more flop out in the sun,
For you're a delicate old bun,
Whose time is soon to come,
My little lop-eared love.

So, sit with me a while,
You bring to me a smile,
I don't want you to leave,
I'll find it hard to breathe,
Let out full unbidden cries,
For you, my little lop-eared love.

Dawn

The trees withstand,
The river flows,
The birds will sing,
A song she knows.

It won't be long,
It won't be slow,
So soon she'll leave,
Her time to go.

The water rushes,
The breeze does too,
They're slowly sinking
With the loss of you.

The clouds grow thick,
Everything greys,
Shedding full silent tears,
They'll be like this for days.

Soon it will stop,
Laughter will flow,
Smiles will emerge,
Love will regrow.

We'll help you heal,
And soothe the pain,
That took deep roots
in sudden rain.

The Trees withstand,
The river flows,
The birds will sing
a song she knows .

It won't be long,
It won't be slow,
So soon she'll leave,
Her time to go.

Young At Heart's Club

My dear, we may be feeble,
Slow and stiffened in our gait,
But we have lived a lot of life,
And will always tell you straight.

Your fitness regimes and diets,
May keep you young today,
But in the winter of your life, my love,
It's the connections that make you stay.

It's seeing Mary at the bingo,
or Fred down at the shops,
It's the weekly young at heart's club,
Where you're not called Gran or Pops.

The day trips down to Sidmouth,
With a wander through the town,
Being social keeps your chin up,
and can stop you feeling down.

Yes, walking keeps you fit,
And eating less bacon is smart,
But I'm telling you my darling,
Gossip's good for your heart.

It's the secret, I'm telling you,
To a long and happy life,
You'll join the young at heart's club,
If you want to stay alive.

Grief

Grief is sat in the front room of someone's house
fussing over cold cups of tea.
It is in the hollow laughter of a family
playing happy for a moment.
It is in the robin that lands nearby.

Sometimes Grief is found at a wedding,
In the middle of a dancefloor it doesn't belong.
Or on a beach where the kids run
like whippets in the surf.
It is a familiar voice from a stranger's tongue.

Grief is a guest that overstays their welcome
when all you want is to be left alone.
It's in the photos on your shelves,
The ring still on your finger.
It is a feather falling from the sky.

Grief will be your life-long companion,
A persistent and agile friend,
Littering your days with reminders,
Reminding you of them.